Resting
IN HIS
Presence

MAKING YOUR
HOME
a haven

A 4-WEEK BIBLE STUDY
ON THE NAMES OF JESUS
by Courtney Joseph Fallick

Welcome to Good Morning Girls! We are so glad you are joining us.

God created us to walk with Him, to know Him, and to be loved by Him. He is our living well, and when we drink from the water He continually provides, His living water will change the entire course of our lives.

> Jesus said: "Whoever drinks of the water that I will give him will never be thirsty again. The water that I will give him will become in him a spring of water welling up to eternal life." ~ John 4:14 (ESV)

So let's begin.

The method we use here at GMG is called the **SOAK** method.

- ❏ **S**—The S stands for *Scripture*—Read the verse of the day. Then choose 1-2 verses and write them out word for word. (There is no right or wrong choice—just let the Holy Spirit guide you.)

- ❏ **O**—The O stands for *Observation*—Look at the verse or verses you wrote out. Write 1 or 2 observations. What stands out to you? What do you learn about the character of God from these verses? Is there a promise, command or teaching?

- ❏ **A**—The A stands for *Application*—Personalize the verses. What is God saying to you? How can you apply them to your life? Are there any changes you need to make or an action to take?

- ❏ **K**—The K stands for *Kneeling in Prayer*—Pause, kneel and pray. Confess any sin God has revealed to you today. Praise God for His word. Pray the passage over your own life or someone you love. Ask God to help you live out your applications.

SOAK God's word into your heart and squeeze every bit of nourishment you can out of each day's scripture reading. Soon you will find your life transformed by the renewing of your mind!

Walk with the King!

Courtney

WomenLivingWell.org, GoodMorningGirls.org

Join the GMG Community

WomenLivingWell.org | GoodMorningGirls.org

Facebook.com/WomenLivingwell | Facebook.com/GoodMorningGirlsWLW

Instagram.com/WomenLivingWell #WomenLivingWell

#MakingYourHomeAHaven

GMG Bible Coloring Chart

COLORS	KEYWORDS
PURPLE	God, Jesus, Holy Spirit, Saviour, Messiah
PINK	women of the Bible, family, marriage, parenting, friendship, relationships
RED	love, kindness, mercy, compassion, peace, grace
GREEN	faith, obedience, growth, fruit, salvation, fellowship, repentance
YELLOW	worship, prayer, praise, doctrine, angels, miracles, power of God, blessings
BLUE	wisdom, teaching, instruction, commands
ORANGE	prophecy, history, times, places, kings, genealogies, people, numbers, covenants, vows, visions, oaths, future
GRAY	Satan, sin, death, hell, evil, idols, false teachers, hypocrisy, temptation

TABLE OF CONTENTS

Introduction

Welcome to the *Making Your Home a Haven* Bible Study! 14 years ago, I began this series on-line at WomenLivingWell.org. Never could I have imagined how much it would resonate with so many women around the world. I pray this study blesses you in the same way!

If you have been feeling disconnected from God or if you have a desire to go deeper in your walk with the Lord, then this study is for you.

God's pace is much slower than this world's pace.

We must slow down to catch up with God.

We must create calm moments in our day because it's in the unhurried moments that we can clearly see and hear the voice of God.

This Bible Study is going to help you slow down. It is going to force you to pause every day and **enter into the presence** of our Almighty God through thanksgiving, prayer and the reading of God's Word.

We are going to take a close look at the names of Jesus and experience him as the Bread of Life, King of Kings, Lord of Lords, Lamb of God, Light of the World, Living Water, Messiah, Redeemer, Savior, Shepherd, Son of God, the Way, the Truth and the Life and so much more!

But we must stop and rest. Because we do not rest, we miss hearing God's voice. Psalm 23 comes to mind. "The Lord is my shepherd; I shall not want. He makes me lie down in green pastures. He leads me beside still waters. He restores my soul. He leads me in paths of righteousness for his name's sake."

Are you experiencing the green pastures, the quiet waters, and the restoration of your soul that Psalm 23 speaks of, from resting with your Shepherd?

Remember how the crowds pressed in on Jesus everywhere He went? Everywhere He turned, there was a need unmet, and though there was so much to do...He withdrew to rest.

Luke 5:16 says, *"But he would withdraw to desolate places and pray."*

If Jesus needed alone time with God, then certainly we do. Just think of the wisdom He wants to impart to you, the strength and the peace you may be missing out on.

Give yourself permission not to have your to-do list all checked off in order for you to rest and get alone with God.

Each week, I will provide for you a practical challenge of something I do in my home that makes it more of a haven. I hope you will take the challenges. They do make a difference!

Each weekday, we will pause, give thanks, pray and meditate on God's Word through SOAKing in the daily scripture reading for the day.

Also, online at *WomenLivingWell.org* you will find 4 videos, one per week, that correspond with the scriptures we are studying.

I pray that your time spent in God's Word will lead you to rest for your soul and release of your burdens, so you can live a life of peace and freedom in Christ no matter what you are facing.

I can't wait to take this journey with you!

Let's get started!

Keep Walking with the King,

Courtney

Week 1

Resting

in His

Presence

WEEK 1 CHALLENGE

Go buy an extra-large candle and light your candle every day in your home. Each time the glimmer of the candle catches your eye, slow down, pray, remember God is with you and rest in his presence.

I will be starting my candle in the morning, but you can start yours at dinnertime or whenever is convenient for you. I will be placing mine in the kitchen—the main hub of my home.

{Share your pictures of your candle on Instagram by using the hashtags: #MakingYourHomeAHaven and #WomenLivingWell}

Things I Am Grateful for This Week:

_____

_____

_____

_____

_____

_____

_____

_____

_____

Things I Am Praying for This Week:

_____

_____

_____

_____

_____

_____

_____

_____

Almighty

"I am the Alpha and the Omega,"
says the Lord God,
"who is and who was and
who is to come, the Almighty."

Revelation 1:8

Revelation 1:8 reminds us that not only is God at the beginning of all things and the end of all things, but he is absolutely and completely sovereign and mighty. He has ultimate control over everything concerning you, both small and great. Nothing is impossible for him because he is Almighty. Are you in a situation right now that seems impossible to resolve? Trust God.

You can rest, even in troubled times, because Almighty God is with you and in control.

Dear God,

Thank you for the peace of knowing that when things feel out of control, you are still in control. You are Almighty, all powerful, and all knowing, and I have no reason to fear. Help me to rest in the knowledge that before situations arise you already have the answer ready and waiting. I cast all my cares upon you today.

You are trustworthy! Amen.

DAY 1
Revelation 1:8

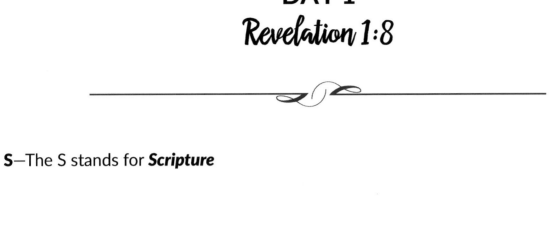

S—The S stands for **Scripture**

O—The O stands for **Observation**

A—The A stands for **Application**

K—The K stands for **Kneeling in Prayer**

Bread of Life
Jesus said to them, "I am the bread of life; whoever comes to me shall not hunger, and whoever believes in me shall never thirst.

John 6:35

Jesus is the Bread of Life. Bread in Bible times was essential to the physical life and Jesus is essential for our spiritual life. He said, "Blessed are those who hunger and thirst for righteousness, for they shall be satisfied." When we hunger for God and his word, his promise is that he will satisfy our hunger with fulness of life that will never go away. God provided manna in the desert so that the Israelites never hungered. Christ is the bread of life for us today to satisfy our soul-hunger. Are you hungry? What are you feeding your soul right now?

You can rest in Jesus free from longing because he is the bread of life.

Dear God,

When the things of this world offer empty promises to bring me contentment, help me remember that only you can satisfy my soul hunger with your bread that gives fulness of life. I pray that as I encounter those who are hungry and thirsty, that you will remind me to share Jesus—the bread of life—with them, so that they never hunger again.

You are my satisfaction! Amen.

DAY 2
John 6:35

S—The S stands for **_Scripture_**

O—The O stands for **_Observation_**

A—The A stands for **_Application_**

K—The K stands for **_Kneeling in Prayer_**

Carpenter

Is not this the carpenter, the son of Mary and brother of James and Joseph and Judas and Simon? And are not his sisters here with us?"
And they took offense at him.

Mark 6:3

The Greek word for carpenter isn't limited to a builder with wood, it also means a craftsman. Whenever a craftsman begins a project, it's not pretty at first. In fact, it can be messy and chaotic, but there is a purpose and vision for his art. Paul says in Ephesians, "For we are his workmanship, created in Christ Jesus for good works, which God prepared beforehand." It can be very discouraging when life gets messy and chaotic; we tend to stop trusting God and try to fix things ourselves. What is Jesus doing in your life right now?

We can rest in Jesus because He is the Carpenter of our life.

Dear God,

When I grow discouraged and frustrated in the messiness and chaos of life, help me to remember that the good work you have begun, you have promised to finish. Help me to trust your capable hands to bring beauty from chaos. Thank you for your promise that you make all things beautiful in your time.

You are my creator! Amen.

DAY 3
Mark 6:3

S—The S stands for *Scripture*

O—The O stands for *Observation*

A—The A stands for *Application*

K—The K stands for *Kneeling in Prayer*

Door

So Jesus again said to them, "Truly, truly, I say to you, I am the door of the sheep. All who came before me are thieves and robbers, but the sheep did not listen to them. I am the door. If anyone enters by me, he will be saved and will go in and out and find pasture.

John 10:7-9

In Jesus' time, shelters were made for sheep with just one door and the shepherd would lay down across the doorway to keep the sheep in and enemies out. This is such a beautiful picture of Jesus laying down his life for us out of love to protect and keep us from the enemy and those who would deceive and lead us astray. We all face times in our life when we feel unloved and rejected. In these times, we can remember that Jesus is the door of the sheep. In what way do you witness Christ's protection in your life right now?

We can rest in Jesus' protection because he is the door.

Dear God,

I am so overwhelmed by the depth of your love for me. It comforts me to know that in those times when I feel unloved, that you have laid down your life to protect and keep me. Help me to always keep my eyes on you.

You are my great protector! Amen.

DAY 4
John 10:7~9

S—The S stands for *Scripture*

O—The O stands for *Observation*

A—The A stands for *Application*

K—The K stands for *Kneeling in Prayer*

Immanuel

Behold, the virgin shall conceive and bear a son, and they shall call his name Immanuel" (which means, God with us).

Matthew 1:23

God chose not to remain distant from mankind, but to come live with us and identify with our suffering. In fact, he made it his name, the very essence of who he is. "God with us." We are truly never alone. God is with us and his promise is that he will never leave us nor forsake us. Everyone has times when they feel lonely; even when surrounded by people. In what ways have you sensed God with you lately?

We can rest in Jesus because he is Immanuel, God with us.

Dear God,

In those times when I feel lonely and forgotten, help me to take my eyes off of me and turn them back to you. I know you are always with me and never leave me, never forsake me, and never forget me. Thank you for always being with me and loving me.

You are faithful and you are my friend. Amen.

DAY 5
Matthew 1:23

S—The S stands for ***Scripture***

O—The O stands for ***Observation***

A—The A stands for ***Application***

K—The K stands for ***Kneeling in Prayer***

Week 2

Resting in His Presence

WEEK 2 CHALLENGE

Keep your candle going and add to it—soft music every day in your home. Choose worship, classical or another form of peaceful music that relaxes you and helps you focus on the Lord and his presence.

My candle and soft music literally change the atmosphere of my home. While the rest of my home may be messy, my candle keeps on burning and my soft music keeps on playing. Morning, noon and night they serve me. My candle serves me with a flickering warm light, a pleasant scent, and a reminder to turn to God as my source of strength and help. My music serves me with a soothing sound. They don't make messes, they don't need managed, they just simply bless me and my family. I hope it blesses you too.

{Share your pictures of your favorite worship CD or playlist on Instagram by using the hashtags: #MakingYourHomeAHaven and #WomenLivingWell}

Things I Am Grateful for This Week:

_____

_____

_____

_____

_____

_____

_____

_____

Things I Am Praying for This Week:

_____

_____

_____

_____

_____

_____

_____

God

For to us a child is born, to us a son is given; and the government shall be upon his shoulder and his name shall be called Wonderful Counselor, Mighty God, Everlasting Father, Prince of Peace.

Isaiah 9:6

Life is filled with enormous challenges that sometimes seem impossible. Jesus promised that with God all things are possible. He went on to prove this promise to be true over and over as he multiplied food, raised the dead, and healed those who had been given up to a lifetime of disease and disability. His promise is still true today. What seems impossible to man is possible with God. What impossible need do you have right now? Surrender it to God.

We can rest in Jesus because he is Mighty God with whom all things are possible.

Dear God,

Help me remember that when life's circumstances seem impossible, they are possible for you. When life feels overwhelming, remind me to turn them over to you, with whom everything is possible. I pray that my trust and faith in you will grow strong as I surrender to you my impossible needs.

You are my rock and mighty fortress! Amen.

DAY 1
Isaiah 9:6

S—The S stands for **Scripture**

O—The O stands for **Observation**

A—The A stands for **Application**

K—The K stands for **Kneeling in Prayer**

King of Kings & Lord of Lords

Then I saw heaven opened, and behold, a white horse! The one sitting on it is called Faithful and True, and in righteousness he judges and makes war. His eyes are like a flame of fire, and on his head are many diadems, and he has a name written that no one knows but himself. He is clothed in a robe dipped in blood, and the name by which he is called is The Word of God. And the armies of heaven, arrayed in fine linen, white and pure, were following him on white horses. From his mouth comes a sharp sword with which to strike down the nations, and he will rule them with a rod of iron. He will tread the winepress of the fury of the wrath of God the Almighty. On his robe and on his thigh he has a name written, King of kings and Lord of lords.

Revelation 19:11-16

It is easy to be frustrated and discouraged when we see our governmental leaders make decisions that are unbiblical and affect our lives negatively. In these times, it helps to remember that God has always protected and redeemed His people. No political ruler is above God's purpose and they only possess power that God grants to them. He is the supreme ruler over all the Universe. In what ways are you praying for your leaders right now?

We can rest in Jesus because he is the King of kings and Lord of lords.

Dear God,

What a comfort it is to know that I don't have to allow what happens on a political level steal my peace and joy, because you are still in control. Your purposes will always prevail, no matter who rises to power. Help me to rest in the truth that you are the King of all kings and the Lord of all lords.

You are victorious over all! Amen.

DAY 2
Revelation 19:11~16

S—The S stands for **Scripture**

O—The O stands for **Observation**

A—The A stands for **Application**

K—The K stands for **Kneeling in Prayer**

Lamb of God

The next day he saw Jesus coming toward him, and said, "Behold, the Lamb of God, who takes away the sin of the world!

John 1:29

Where the blood of a lamb was inadequate to completely remove man's sin, the Lamb of God, Jesus' blood, would completely remove sin and pardon mankind. The psalmist said that God removes our sin from us "as far as the east is from the west". We no longer have to live under the condemnation of our sin. We have been pardoned! In what ways are you struggling with condemnation from your past sin right now?

We can rest in Jesus, for he is the Lamb of God, who takes away the sin of the world.

Dear God,

There are times when I remember things from my past and feel shame and condemnation that I know isn't from you. When the enemy reminds me of my past, help me to remember that my sin is removed and I have been pardoned by the blood of the Lamb. Help me remember that you don't see that sin any longer, and that that by your blood I am a new creation. The old is gone and the new has come. Thank you that you have given me new life.

You are a forgiving, faithful Father! Amen.

DAY 3
John 1:29

S—The S stands for **Scripture**

O—The O stands for **Observation**

A—The A stands for **Application**

K—The K stands for **Kneeling in Prayer**

Light of the World

Jesus spoke to them, saying,
"I am the light of the world.
Whoever follows me will not walk in
darkness, but will have the light of life."

John 8:12

There is so much deception and distortion in our culture that it is hard to know what is truth and what is a lie. Searching for truth in all of the usual places leaves us fumbling in the dark. As children of God, we don't have to fumble in the dark, because Jesus is our light. When we follow Christ, we no longer walk in darkness. His light illuminates our path so we can live with confidence and stability in the midst of an unstable and fluid society. What are you doing right now to make sure you continue walking in the light?

We can rest in Jesus because he is the light of the world.

Dear God,

When the confusion of this culture of disinformation crowds in, help me to remember to keep my eyes on you—the light of the world. May your light shine brightly through me so that those around me who are fumbling in the darkness will see your light in me and find the truth that will set them free.

You are the only truth we need! Amen.

DAY 4
John 8:12

S—The S stands for **Scripture**

O—The O stands for **Observation**

A—The A stands for **Application**

K—The K stands for **Kneeling in Prayer**

Living Water

Jesus said to her, "Everyone who drinks of this water will be thirsty again, but whoever drinks of the water that I will give him will never be thirsty again. The water that I will give him will become in him a spring of water welling up to eternal life."

John 4:13~14

When we are thirsty, we quench our thirst with fresh water. But it's not as easy to quench the thirst we feel in our soul. There is only one source that can quench our soul thirst, and that is Jesus the Living Water. His water fills us, and becomes a gyser of eternal life so that we can be His ministers to those around us. How has Jesus quenched your soul thirst lately? Share a recent testimony.

We can rest in Jesus because he is the Living Water.

Dear God,

Thank you that you give us your life in abundance, more than what we could ask or think. Help me to be a vessel of honor so that your life can flow through me to those around me who need the Living Water to quench their soul thirst.

You are my everlasting supply! Amen.

DAY 5
John 4:13-14

S—The S stands for **Scripture**

O—The O stands for **Observation**

A—The A stands for **Application**

K—The K stands for **Kneeling in Prayer**

Resting

in His

Presence

WEEK 3 CHALLENGE

Go pick a bouquet of flowers from your garden or a nearby field or buy yourself a small bouquet. Each time you see the flowers, be reminded of God's love and presence with you. Our creator God is with you and listening to your prayers.

I will be purchasing a small bouquet from my grocery store and placing it in a vase, in my kitchen.

{Share your pictures of your flowers on Instagram by using the hashtags: #MakingYourHomeAHaven and #WomenLivingWell}

Things I Am Grateful for This Week:

_____

_____

_____

_____

_____

_____

_____

_____

Things I Am Praying for This Week:

_____

_____

_____

_____

_____

_____

_____

Man of Sorrows

He was despised and rejected by men, a man of sorrows and acquainted with grief; and as one from whom men hide their faces he was despised, and we esteemed him not.

Isaiah 53:3

No one is exempt from sorrow. At some point in our life, we're touched by sorrow; some more deeply than others. God wants you to know that he is not removed from you in your sorrow. He is so intimately acquainted with sorrow that Christ is called "Man of Sorrows". He knows the grief of rejection and being despised, misunderstood, and disrespected. He bore that pain so that you don't have to hide from him in your sorrow. Are you struggling with sorrow right now?

You can rest in Jesus because he is a Man of Sorrows.

Dear God,

In times of sorrow, remind me that you went through grief, rejection, and sorrow. Remind me that I can trust that you not only know my pain, but that you can heal my broken heart. You see *me*, and you care. Thank you that your mercy is new every morning and that your love is never-ending.

You are my closest friend! Amen.

DAY 1
Isaiah 53:3

S—The S stands for ***Scripture***

O—The O stands for ***Observation***

A—The A stands for ***Application***

K—The K stands for ***Kneeling in Prayer***

Messiah

He first found his own brother Simon and said to him, "We have found the Messiah" (which means Christ).

John 1:41

Messiah is Hebrew for Christ, which means the anointed one. On the Sabbath day in the Synanogue, Jesus stood up and read from Isaiah 61, "The Spirit of the Lord God is upon me, because the Lord has anointed me to bring good news to the poor…" Being anointed was a sign of being set apart for a special purpose. The Messiah, came to earth for a special purpose, to bring the gospel to mankind and to be the final sacrifice for sin. Now he wants to work that special purpose through us. In what way are you allowing the Messiah to bring the gospel through you?

We can rest in Jesus because He is Messiah.

Dear God,

It's not easy living in this fallen world, surrounded by sin, brokenness, and pain. Thank you that you are the Messiah and you love us. You came to set us free from our sin. Help me to see others as you see them and guide me to those who need to be set free too.

You are a loving Savior! Amen.

DAY 2
John 1:41

S—The S stands for **Scripture**

O—The O stands for **Observation**

A—The A stands for **Application**

K—The K stands for **Kneeling in Prayer**

Redeemer

For I know that my Redeemer lives, and at the last he will stand upon the earth.

Job 19:25

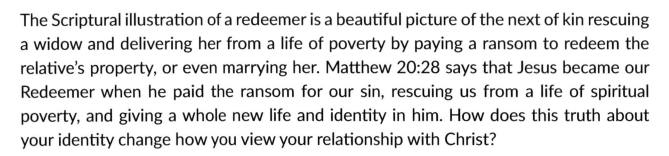

The Scriptural illustration of a redeemer is a beautiful picture of the next of kin rescuing a widow and delivering her from a life of poverty by paying a ransom to redeem the relative's property, or even marrying her. Matthew 20:28 says that Jesus became our Redeemer when he paid the ransom for our sin, rescuing us from a life of spiritual poverty, and giving a whole new life and identity in him. How does this truth about your identity change how you view your relationship with Christ?

We can rest in Jesus because he is our Redeemer.

Dear God,

When the enemy tries to steal my peace and joy, help me remember the great work you did for me when you redeemed me from a life of sin and spiritual poverty. Thank you for giving me a new life, new name, and new identity in you. Help me never take for granted your great sacrifice for me.

You are my greatest joy! Amen.

DAY 3
Job 19:25

S—The S stands for **Scripture**

O—The O stands for **Observation**

A—The A stands for **Application**

K—The K stands for **Kneeling in Prayer**

Resurrection and the Life

Jesus said to her,
"I am the resurrection and
the life. Whoever believes in me,
though he die, yet shall he live.

John 11:25

The holiday season is a difficult time for many because during the holidays we gather as a family more intentionally, so we miss our loved ones who have gone on before us even more. It's easy to get overwhelmed by the grief of loss, just as Mary did with the loss of her brother Lazarus. Jesus comforted her when he spoke these words: "I am the resurrection and the life." We can have hope because he is our resurrecton and he does not just resurrect us but he is life. Are you grieving over a loss? How does Jesus being the Resurrection and the Life give you comfort today?

We can rest in Jesus because he is the Resurrection and the Life.

Dear God,

When my heart is filled with the sorrow of loss, help me remember that in you there is no death. In you is only life. May I find comfort in you on the hard days, knowing that you are our resurrection and life and that one day soon I will be together with my loved ones once more. My hope is in you.

You are my comforter! Amen.

DAY 4
John 11:25

S—The S stands for **Scripture**

O—The O stands for **Observation**

A—The A stands for **Application**

K—The K stands for **Kneeling in Prayer**

Savior

And the angel said to them, "Fear not, for behold, I bring you good news of great joy that will be for all the people. For unto you is born this day in the city of David a Savior, who is Christ the Lord.

Luke 2:10-11

Man can't save himself. If we could save ourselves from addiction, depression, guilt, or any other thing that plagues mankind, we would. The fact is that deep inside all of mankind is a brokenness so deep that only God can save and deliver. God is so full of love and grace that he sent his Son to save us. Salvation in any other form was completely unattainable. We can't earn it and we don't deserve it, but he sent his only Son as our Savior because he loves us. In what way does Jesus being your Savior bring comfort to you and bring you joy?

We can rest in Jesus because he is our Savior.

Dear God,

All of my attempts to change myself have failed miserably. I know that I can't free or change myself. You are my Savior and you can do what no man can do. On those days when I feel helpless, remind me that you are my Savior and what is impossible with man is possible with you. Salvation is in your name alone.

You are all-powerful and yet you love me! Amen.

DAY 5
Luke 2:10~11

S—The S stands for **Scripture**

O—The O stands for **Observation**

A—The A stands for **Application**

K—The K stands for **Kneeling in Prayer**

Resting in His Presence

WEEK 4 CHALLENGE

Seek out a place of solitude to get alone with God. Stop your work, turn off your phone, the television, music and computer. Be still. Practice the presence of God. Go outside or find a place in your home, where you can be alone and simply rest and be at peace with the Lord.

Rest is a need—not a want. Rest is not optional or something we wait to do when we are retired. Rest is a blessing from the Lord, and it requires humility to admit we need it. I'll be running a bubble bath and probably taking a much-needed nap this week. Soul care is self-care. So, enjoy it.

{Share your pictures of your favorite place to rest on Instagram by using the hashtags: #MakingYourHomeAHaven and #WomenLivingWell}

Things I Am Grateful for This Week:

_____

_____

_____

_____

_____

_____

_____

Things I Am Praying for This Week:

_____

_____

_____

_____

_____

_____

_____

_____

Shepherd

I am the good shepherd.
The good shepherd lays down
his life for the sheep.

John 10:11

A good shepherd leads his sheep to find nourishment and rest. His rod and staff protect and rescue them from danger. In Bible times, the shepherd would lay across the door of the sheep pen to protect the sheep from predators, literally laying his life down for his sheep. Many people today battle a crippling feeling of helplessness and loneliness. Jesus is our good Shepherd. He will never leave you. He cares for every need you have. He is protecting you from the enemy's attack. Are you trying to do life on your own right now? In what area of your life are you struggling to trust Jesus as your Shepherd?

We can rest in Jesus because he is our Shepherd.

Dear God,

When I feel alone and helpless, help me remember that you are always with me. Help me remember that I do not have to handle life alone, but that Jesus – my Shepherd – is with me, guiding me, protecting me, and providing for everything I need.
You are my faithful provider! Amen.

DAY 1
John 10:11

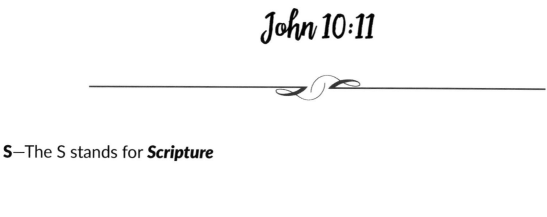

S—The S stands for ***Scripture***

O—The O stands for ***Observation***

A—The A stands for ***Application***

K—The K stands for ***Kneeling in Prayer***

Son of God

And the angel answered her, "The Holy Spirit will come upon you, and the power of the Most High will overshadow you; therefore the child to be born will be called holy the Son of God.

Luke 1:35

Do you struggle with understanding and accepting God's unfailing love? The Son of God came as the visual reprentation of God's love. He said, "Whoever has seen me has seen the Father." God loved us so much that he did what no other god in any other religion has ever done. He sent his son in human form, limited his diety, lived among mankind, and then offered himself as a sacrifice for their sin. He loves us so much! How does this truth change how you view Jesus' love for you today?

We can rest in Jesus because he is the Son of God.

Dear God,

I know your love for me is unending, even when I don't always do things the right way. When I'm feeling condemnation, help me remember that before I even accepted you as my Savior, you loved me and died for me. You sent your only Son to die in my place.

You are a loving Father! Amen.

DAY 2
Luke 1:35

S—The S stands for *Scripture*

O—The O stands for *Observation*

A—The A stands for *Application*

K—The K stands for *Kneeling in Prayer*

The Vine

*I am the vine; you are the branches.
Whoever abides in me and I in him,
he it is that bears much fruit, for apart
from me you can do nothing.*

John 15:5

Without a vine, branches have no source of nourishment. No fruit will grow and they will die. Jesus is our vine. He is our source of life and spiritual nourishment. Without him we cannot bear fruit in our lives. How connected are you to Jesus the vine? Are you receiving daily nourishment from him? Is your life bearing fruit? What can you start doing right now to abide in him more consistently?

We can rest in Jesus because he is the vine.

Dear God,

You are the source of all life, and this truth gives me great peace. When all of the chaos of life saps my strength and leaves me feeling weak, help me remember to look to the only source of life, Jesus the Vine. I want to abide in you and your word so that I can grow, flourish and bear abundant fruit in you.

You are my life! Amen.

DAY 3

John 15:5

S—The S stands for *Scripture*

O—The O stands for *Observation*

A—The A stands for *Application*

K—The K stands for *Kneeling in Prayer*

The Way, the Truth, and the Life

Jesus said to him, "I am the way, and the truth, and the life. No one comes to the Father except through me."

John 14:6

Many today are wondering what is the right path. They ask themselves, "What is truth?". They question the meaning of life. The answer to all of these is found in Jesus. He *is* the way, he *is* the truth and he *is* the life. He is the answer for every question and need of mankind. How has Jesus put to rest these questions in your heart? Share your testimony with someone today.

We can rest in Jesus because he is the way, the truth and the life.

Dear God,

Thank you, Lord that you are the answer for every question and need in my heart. Thank you that we don't have to stumble around to find our way in this confusing world, but that knowing you, we can know the way, know the truth, and know life. Give me an opportunity to share this wonderful news with someone today.

You are my life! Amen.

DAY 4
John 14:6

S—The S stands for **Scripture**

O—The O stands for **Observation**

A—The A stands for **Application**

K—The K stands for **Kneeling in Prayer**

The Word

And the Word became flesh and dwelt among us, and we have seen his glory, glory as of the only Son from the Father, full of grace and truth.

John 1:14

Have you ever felt you needed a word from God; a direct word to speak to your present situation? The Bible says that Jesus is the very Word of God. He came as the physical representation of the power and wisdom of God. When we feel uncertain and confused, the Word brings clarity and direction. That's why James said that if we lack wisdom, all we need to do is ask and God will give it to us. We simply need ears to hear what the Word is saying. How well have you been listening to Word lately?

We can rest in Jesus because he is the word.

Dear God,

When life is chaotic and messy, and I feel uncertain and confused by what is happening around me, help me remember that your Word can bring clarity and wisdom to every situation. Remind me that the Word is sufficient for everything I face. Help me to hear your voice clearly.

You are the source of all wisdom! Amen.

DAY 5

John 1:14

S—The S stands for **Scripture**

O—The O stands for **Observation**

A—The A stands for **Application**

K—The K stands for **Kneeling in Prayer**

Video Notes

(go to WomenLivingWell.org to find the weekly corresponding videos)

Made in the USA
Las Vegas, NV
26 October 2023